Right@Sight Grade 6

Based on
Read and Play
(original and new series) by
T. A. Johnson

Revised by Caroline Evans

With additional material by Paul Terry

London · Frankfurt · Leipzig · New York

Peters Edition Limited
Hinrichsen House
10–12 Baches Street
London
N1 6DN

First published 2001
© 2001 by Hinrichsen Edition, Peters Edition Limited, London

All rights reserved. No part of this publication may be
reproduced, stored in a retrieval system or transmitted
in any form or by any means, electronic, mechanical,
photocopying, recording or otherwise, without the
prior written permission of the publisher.

Music-setting and typesetting by Musonix

Cover design by Nick Wakelin
Cover layout and typography by adamhaydesign.com
Text design by c eye, London
Printed in Great Britain by Caligraving Limited
Thetford, Norfolk

Set in Monotype Garamond 3 and Frutiger

Right@Sight

Grade 6

A note to teachers

Sight-reading is one of the most important skills for any musician, and certainly not to be seen as a chore necessary only for passing exams! Right@Sight will help to develop and improve that skill, providing a structured approach and opportunities for regular practice. Hints are provided for the earlier pieces to focus attention on notation, form, texture, interpretation and technique, prompted with questions (left-hand column) and information (right). These should also help to encourage greater musical awareness in all of a student's performing.

In an examination, half a minute will be given to prepare the sight-reading, and the examiner is likely to remind candidates that they may play the music during this time. Encourage your students to try out the opening, the ending and any awkward-looking passages so that they are well prepared before the test starts. Instil careful attention to the fundamental elements of Time, Rhythm and Key – though the key signature comes first on the staff, it is often the first piece of information to be forgotten in performance!

Becoming a good sight-reader needs daily practice, and regular 'exercise' with Right@Sight will prepare students to tackle whatever music they may want to play. Towards the end of the section with commentary, some pieces go a little beyond the standard expected for the grade, so as to stretch players' ability and enable them to face any sight-reading test with increased confidence: to play it right – at sight!

Caroline Evans

Key to symbols

1	Exercise number
T	Time
R	Rhythm
K	Key
?	Questions

Contents

Section 1: Getting started 4

Section 2: On your own now … 23

Section 3: Glossary of musical terms and symbols . . . 40

Right@Sight

Getting started

1 Follow the TRaK

T What is the time signature?

R Can you tap the rhythm of the opening bars?

K Is the key major or minor?

? What harmonic interval frequently occurs in the RH part of this piece?

How should you play the left hand chords in bars 1, 2, 3, 9 and 10?

Are there any changes of hand position?

Notice the small rhythmic variation in bar 10.

The opening is rather modal but name the key in the final bars.

When you play the slurred couplets, drop the wrist slightly on the first chord and raise it gently on the second.

Make sure that the chords are played on the beat and are spread quietly and evenly.

Legato pedalling is required, releasing then depressing the sustaining pedal at the beginning of each bar (but twice in bar 4). Observe the *fermata* (pause) in bar 15. Play gracefully and simply. Look ahead.

TRaK

[R] Can you find all the triplet figures?

[?] How would you describe the texture of this piece?

What sort of mood is suggested by *Lento (Dolce)* and the dynamic range of the piece?

Pace the triplets evenly, making sure that the speed of the 'pulsating' left-hand crotchets does not vary.

Notice how the chordal bass supports the melody line above throughout most of the piece. In the last two bars the left hand plays gently flowing broken chords.

Hold the minims in bars 4 and 10 (RH) while playing the crotchets above or below.

Use the pedal judiciously. Look at the phrasing, dynamics and fingering before you begin.

3

[T] What is quintuple time?

[R] Tap the rhythm of the opening bars.

[K] What is the key?

[?] Can you find any scale passages?

Can you find all the tied notes?

Note the change of time signature in bar 11.

There are two accidentals in bar 3 (RH) which are cancelled in bar 4. The naturals are inserted as a reminder.

The first half of the piece consists mainly of intervals of a third (RH). There are also some fourths and sixths.

Take care with the tied Ds in bars 12–13 (RH). These should be held lightly while playing the quavers below.

It is important to keep counting as you play this piece, emphasizing slightly the first beat of the bar.
As usual, observe the phrasing and all the dynamics. Notice that the left hand is in the treble clef in bars 9–10.

T	What is the time signature?	Note the value of the beat.
R		Tap the rhythm of the opening bars.
K	What is the key of the piece?	Look at the cadence in the last two bars to confirm the key. Find any accidentals.
?	Can you find several harmonic intervals of a sixth?	Notice the harmonic writing in parallel thirds for the the scale passage in bars 5–7 (RH).
	How should you play the slurred couplets (see No. 1)?	The rhythm of bar 15 (RH) is similar to the pattern used in bars 1, 3, 5 and elsewhere, but with the important difference that its second note must be sustained and should not be followed by a rest.

Use the sustaining pedal and play very gracefully. Do not stop. Keep your eyes looking ahead to the next bar.

5

T The piece begins on an upbeat. What is another term for this?

R The piece is based largely on this rhythmic figure (RH). Can you tap this a few times?

K What is the key?

? Can you name the intervals in bar 6 (RH)?

Can you find the changes in clef (LH)?

Count the silent beats before you play the first two semiquavers (RH).

The bass accompaniment in bars 1 and 2 will need care. Tap the left hand alone for these two bars.

Note the accidentals, especially F♭ in bar 8 (LH).

In bars 6 and 10, hold the dotted minim (LH) while playing the quavers above.

Check for any changes of hand position.

Use the sustaining pedal carefully so that the harmonies do not blur. Observe the phrasing, dynamics and fingering. Remember the D♭ in the key signature!

| T | What do you understand by the term simple time?

| R | Can you tap the rhythm of the first four bars a few times?

What is the name of the grace note printed in small type in bars 7 and 14 (LH)?

| K | Are there any key changes during the piece?

| ? | What do you notice about the scale passages in bars 1 and 2?

Is the ascending scale passage in bars 12–13 harmonic or melodic minor?

From bar 10 onwards (LH), contrast the triplets with the dotted rhythm.

These grace notes should be as short as possible.

Look at bars 7–10.

Compare bars 1 and 2 with bars 5 and 6 and note any differences.

The RH melody in bar 15 is based on the descending melodic minor scale of G minor.

Observe the dynamics and phrasing, making a clear difference between the staccato and slurred notes.
Be ready for the changes of clef in bars 13 and 14 (LH).

7

T
R

K Is the key major or minor?

? Can you name the cadence in bar 4?

There are changes of clef for both hands in this piece. Can you find them all?

Check the time signature, as usual.

Always count very evenly, taking particular care over the rhythm in bar 5, where the left hand enters after a quaver rest on the first beat.

Note that bars 1–3 (RH) comprise a series of descending chords in first inversion.

The final perfect cadence should be very delicate.

Aim for vivid contrasts between the passages requiring staccato and slurred articulation. Keep your eyes moving ahead to help you achieve continuity in performance.

[T] Is this piece in duple metre or quadruple metre?

Decide whether you want to count two crotchets or four quavers per bar.

[R] Can you sing or clap the first four bars (RH)?

Notice that the rhythm of bar 1 occurs several times throughout the piece.

[K] What is the key of this piece?

The imperfect cadence in bars 3–4 and the perfect cadence at the end will help you identify the key.

[?] What is meant by the sign ✖ in bars 6, 10 and 19?

Notice that several of the accidentals (E♯, B♯ and F✖) require you to play 'white' notes, not 'black' notes.

What do you notice occurs on the last quaver beat of bar 12?

When natural and chromatically altered versions of the same note appear simultaneously or in close proximity in two different parts of the music (such as the LH and RH of bar 12) the effect is known as a 'false relation'.

Play at a steady pace, without rushing, and bring out the contrasts in articulation and dynamics.

9 Follow the TRaK

Do any changes of key occur?

How should you perform the *tenuto* (𝅘𝅥̄) notes?

What is the meaning of **sfz** in bar 15?

Can you find the clef changes?

Look for any accidentals and notice the modulating sequence in bars 12–15.

Give the meaning of *tenuto*.

Accented notes (𝅘𝅥>) require more attack than tenuto (𝅘𝅥̄) notes.

Practise the change of hand position required in bars 8–9 (both hands).

Try to hear the melody in your head before playing. Play steadily and elegantly.

TRaK

 Do you notice the number of small scale patterns in both hands, including a short chromatic passage in bar 20?

There are several accidentals in this piece.

Find some examples of imitation.

Be prepared for the quick changes of hand position bars 21–24 (RH) and bars 23–24 (LH).

This should be played *Presto* (fast) so there will be no time to look down at the keyboard! Try to keep your eyes looking ahead to the next bar. Remember to play the final bars *fortissimo*.

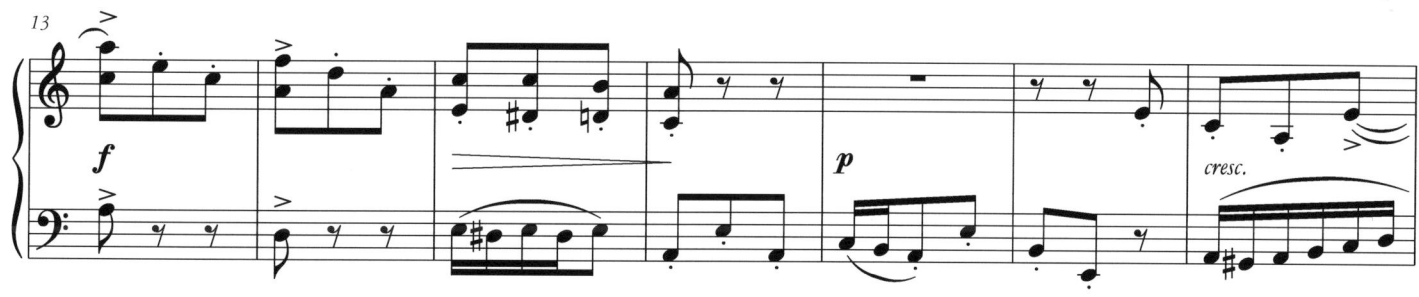

11

- [T] Is the time simple or compound?
- [R] Can you tap the rhythm of the first three bars (both hands)?
- [K] Is the key major or minor?
- [?] What do you notice when you compare bars 1–2 with bars 8–9?
- Can you find all the tied notes?

Note the change of time signature in bar 7.

Keep counting evenly in bars 10–11, taking care not to speed up at this point.

There are modulations to related keys in bars 4–6.

Notice the three-bar phrase in bars 1–3.

Make sure that the tied notes are held for their full value.

Briefly release the sustaining pedal before each change of chord. Note that the pedal is essential in bars 10 and 11, but is better not used in bars 12 and 13. Observe the dynamics and 'sing' out (*cantabile*) the melody.
Play in a gently flowing manner.

TRaK

? Which pedal is indicated by the direction *una corda* in bar 14?

Una corda means one string – on some pianos the key mechanism shifts so that only one string is struck by the hammers when this pedal is pressed. On other pianos the pedal produces a similar effect by damping the strings with a felt mute. The direction *tre corde* (three strings) is an instruction to release the pedal.

What does the abbreviation *sub.* (bar 6) mean?

The change in dynamic should be emphasized by a short break in the pulse, indicated by the commas at the end of bar 5. A similar break occurs in bar 14, just before the final phrase.

Which hand has the melody in bars 9–11?

Make sure that the accompaniment is a little quieter than this melody.

Keep to a steady tempo, but notice that the time signature implies a sense of two, not four, beats in a bar. Dynamics should be precisely observed.

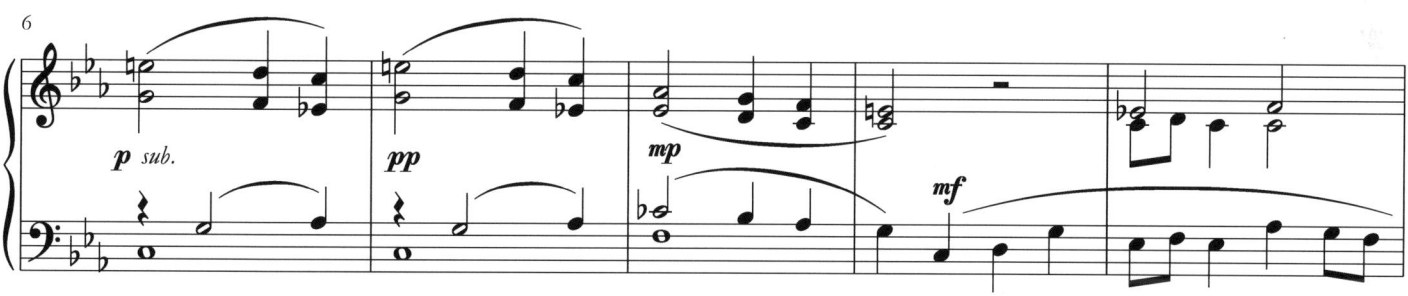

13 TRaK

? What do you notice about the phrase structure?

Do you notice the ascending sequence in bars 6–9, both hands?

What do you notice when you compare bar 13 with bar 14?

Can you find all the examples of notes which should be held while others are played above or below?

The piece begins with two five-bar phrases.

Also note the descending sequence in bars 11–13, both hands.

Bars 15 and 16 use a variant of the figure first heard in bars 1 and 2 of the piece.

Be prepared for the changes of tempo indicated in bars 7, 10 and 14. The first two should be gradual but the third should be more sudden.

Follow all performance instructions and use the sustaining pedal throughout the piece. Play slowly and solemnly (*Adagio solenne*). Finally, remember **all** the sharps in the key signature.

T What do you understand by the term compound time?

R Can you tap the following rhythm? Most of the bars are based on this rhythm.

K Is the key major or minor? The E♯ in bar 2 will help you to determine the key. So too, will the key-note in the last bar.

? What do you notice when you compare bar 5 with bar 6, particularly in the left hand? Name the cadence in bar 2, then name the key and the cadence in bar 7.

Are there any clef changes? Find the bars where the clef returns to its original place.

Ensure that the notes are evenly played as one hand takes over from the other in the ascending quaver passage in bars 11–12. Contrast the *pianissimo* here with a strong *forte* finish. Play lightly (*leggiero*) and not too quickly.

15

[T] What is the value of the beat?

[R] Can you tap the first two bars; and bar 10?

[K] Is the key major or minor?

Are there any key changes?

[?] In bars 1–4, do you notice how the crotchets form the melody while the semiquavers supply a light accompaniment?

Be prepared for the change of rhythm in bar 10.

Note the use of E♮.

Look at bars 5 and 6. Also notice the use of a chromatic note (C♭) in bar 8 (RH).

Play the semiquaver groups in bars 1–4 as block chords:

Give the crotchets a little extra tone and play the semiquavers *legato*.

In bars 10–11 (LH), can you note the change from the 5th to the 2nd finger while holding the tied C?

What is the meaning of *meno mosso*?

Be prepared for any change of hand position as a result of a change of clef.

Note that the A♮ in bar 12 creates a *tierce de Picardie*.

....

Listen carefully when using the sustaining pedal and play in a *cantabile* style with a good strong tone.

[T]

[R] Can you tap the rhythm of the first two bars?

[K] Is the key major or minor?

Are there any key changes?

[?] What do you notice when you compare bars 1 and 2 with bars 11 and 12?

In which clef does the left hand begin?

Can you find all the tied notes?

This piece is in quintuple time.

As you tap, count 5 beats in each bar, thinking in a combination of 3 and 2.

Check the accidentals.

Look at bars 6 and 7.

Notice the small scale passages throughout the piece (LH).

Note all the clef changes.

Give the tied notes their full value. The same applies to all the dotted minims.

Play at a moderate speed in a simple flowing manner, observing the five-bar phrases.

17

T How many beats are there in a bar?

R Ensure that the semiquavers in bars 6 and 7 (RH) and in bar 14 (LH) are timed correctly.

K Are there any changes of key?

Check for accidentals.

Which hand has the melody in bars 9 and 10?

Identify the chord in the first half of bar 13.

Can you find all the changes of clef?

Notice that the last note (RH) is in the bass clef.

Look at bar 14 (RH) and see which notes are tied and which are slurred.

Play very smoothly, using the pedal to help sustain the sound through the wide leaps, and with a good *cantabile* tone.

[T] Are there any changes of time signature?

[R] Can you look carefully at the rhythm in bars 1 and 2? This rhythm, duplets against triplets, appears often throughout the piece.

[K] What is the key?

[?] Can you perform the slurred duplets so that the tone is lighter on the second note?

What effect does the C♯ have on the last two chords?

Keep counting.

The rhythm produced by:

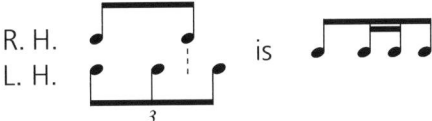

Tap this several times.

Check all accidentals.

In bars 7–8, and bars 14 and 15, see that the quavers are played evenly as one hand takes over from the other.

Give the French term for this.

Observe all the phrasing and dynamics. Play slowly (*Lento*) and expressively.

19

[T] How many beats are there in a bar?

[R] Can you find all the places where this rhythm occurs?

This piece is in the style of a Charleston, a lively popular dance of the 1920s.

Can you make sure that the tied notes are held for their full value?

Tap the first four bars a number of times, hands together. Note the subtle change to this rhythm from bar 9 onwards.

Also note the dotted rhythm in bars 2, 6, 8 and 10 (LH), and play with precision.

[K] What is the key?

Find the notes chromatic to the key.

[?] Can you find all the clef changes (LH)?

Perform the *staccato* notes brightly and lightly, as if played *pizzicato* by a double bass. This piece should be played quickly and rhythmically.

Right@Sight

On your own now …

The following pieces do not have hints to help. Give yourself half a minute to try out any difficult-looking passages and decide on the character of the music. Then play through each piece without stopping. Remember that the most important thing is to keep to a regular pulse, without hesitating, and to keep going. Don't stop to correct mistakes. For a really good mark in the exam you will be expected to observe the expressive details and to give the music a sense of shape and purpose.

Remember … follow the TRaK , look ahead, keep counting and keep going!

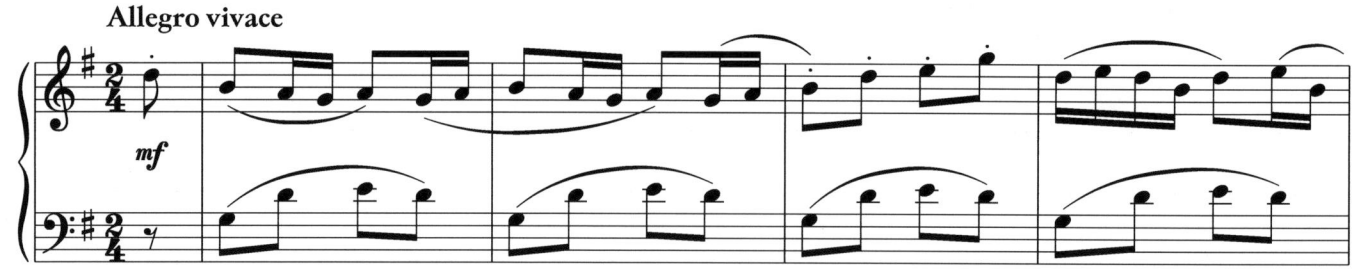

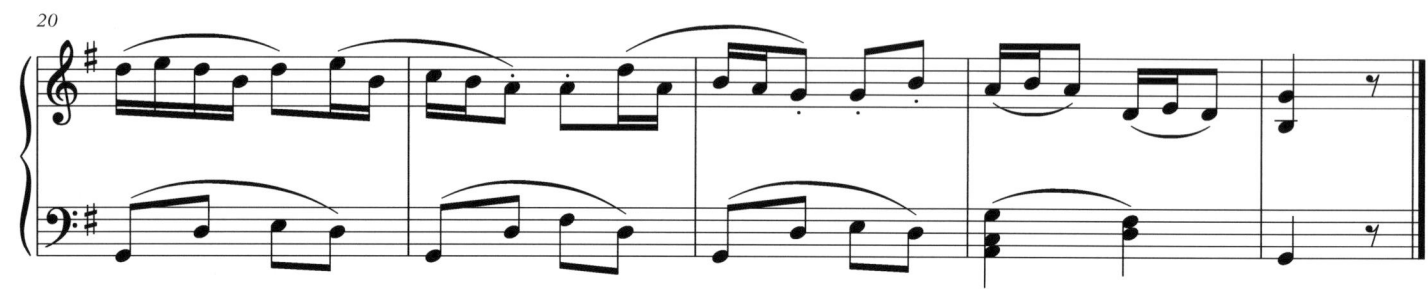

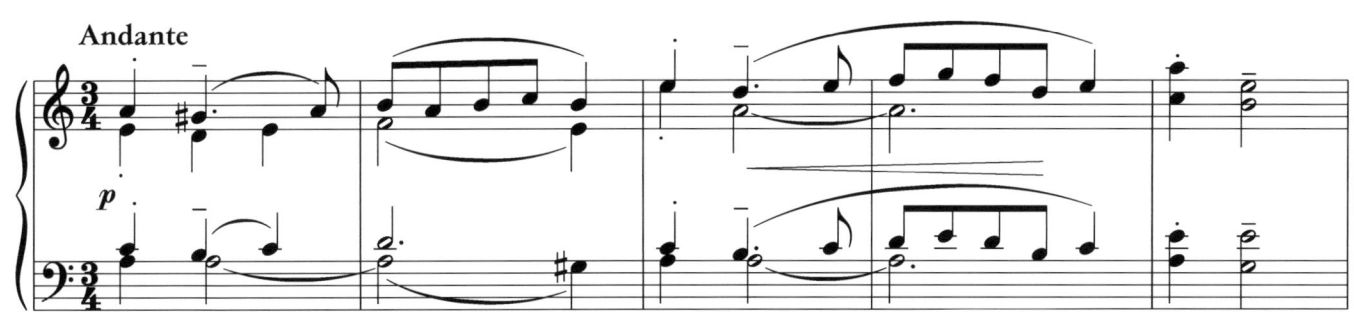

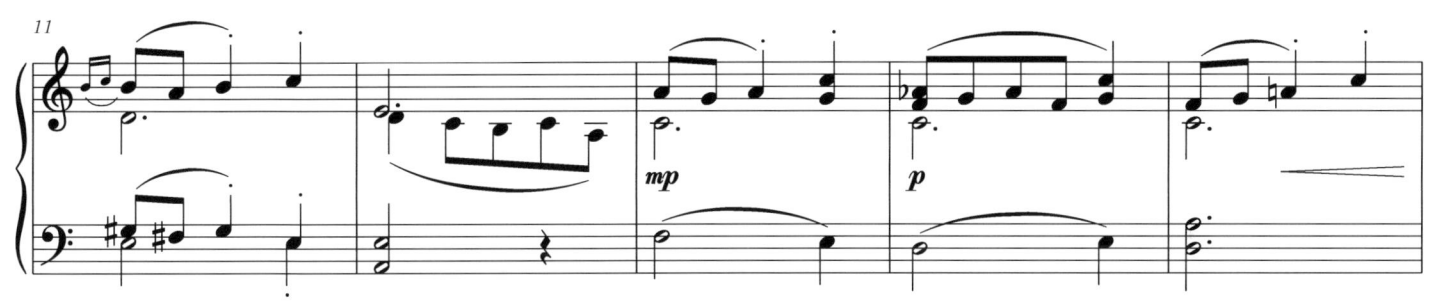

Glossary of musical terms and symbols

A tempo	Return to the original speed
Accelerando	Gradually becoming faster
Adagio	Slowly
Allegretto	Fairly quick, not as fast as *Allegro*
Allegro	(*lit.* cheerful) Quick, lively
Anacrusis	An upbeat
Andante	Walking pace; moderate speed
Cantabile	In a singing style
Con pedale (ped.)	Use the sustaining pedal
Crescendo, cresc.	Gradually becoming louder
Diminuendo; dim.	Gradually becoming quieter
Dolce	Sweet
Grazioso	Gracefully
Legato	Smooth
Leggiero	Light
Lento	Slow
Meno mosso	Less movement; not so fast
Moderato	Moderate speed
Poco	Little
Presto	Fast (faster than *Allegro*)
Rallentando; rall.	Gradually becoming slower
Ritardando; ritard.; rit.	Gradually getting slower
Ritenuto; rit.	Held back
Semplice	In a simple, unaffected style
Sforzando, sforzato, **sfz**, **sf**	Accented, forced
Solenne	Solemn
Spiritoso	In a spirited manner
Staccato	Detached
Subito, sub.	Suddenly
Tempo di gavotta	In the time (and style) of a gavotte
Tempo di marcia	In the time (and style) of a march
Tempo di menuetto	In the time (and style) of a minuet
Tempo primo	Return to original speed
Tenuto; ten.	Held (♩ ♩)
Tierce de Picardie	*Fr.* Picardy third, a major third in the tonic chord at the end of a piece in a minor key
Tre corde	(*lit.* Three strings); release the left pedal
Una corda	(*lit.* One string); press the left pedal
Vivace	Lively, quick
𝄐 (Fermata)	Pause
♪ (Acciaccatura)	A 'crushed' note, played as quickly as possible
8va - - - - - -	(It. *ottava*) Play an octave higher
(Mezzo-staccato)	Semi-staccato, slight degree of separation